A Head Full of Notions

A Head Full of Notions

A Story about Robert Fulton

by Andy Russell Bowen
illustrations by Lisa Harvey

A Carolrhoda Creative Minds Book

Carolrhoda Books, Inc./Minneapolis

*For Edgar, who first taught me about rivers
and boats*

Text copyright © 1997 by Andy Russell Bowen
Illustrations copyright © 1997 by Lisa Harvey

This book is available in two editions:
Library binding by Carolrhoda Books, Inc.
Soft cover by First Avenue Editions
c/o The Lerner Group
241 First Avenue North
Minneapolis, Minnesota 55401

Library of Congress Cataloging-in-Publication Data

Bowen, Andy Russell.
    A head full of notions : a story about Robert Fulton / by Andy Russell
Bowen ; illustrations by Lisa Harvey.
        p.   cm. — (A Carolrhoda creative minds book)
    Includes bibliographical references and index.
    Summary: Describes the life and work of the talented inventor and re-
sourceful businessman, with special emphasis on his development of the
steamboat.
    ISBN 0-87614-876-3 (lib. bdg.)
    ISBN 1-57505-026-9 (pbk.)
    1. Fulton, Robert, 1765–1815—Juvenile literature. 2. Marine engineers—
United States—Biography—Juvenile literature. 3. Inventors—United States—
Biography—Juvenile literature. [1. Fulton, Robert, 1765–1815. 2. Inventors.
3. Steamboats—History.] I. Harvey, Lisa, ill. II. Title. III. Series.
VM140.F9B69   1996
623.8'24'092—dc20
[B]   96-5752

Manufactured in the United States of America
1 2 3 4 5 6 – MA – 02 01 00 99 98 97

Table of Contents

① Quicksilver Bob

Fresh out of patience, the teacher barked at young Fulton to pay attention. The boy's mind was wandering again. Nine-year-old Robert grumbled, corrected his posture, and refocused his eyes on the lesson in front of him.

That day was going to be like so many others. Robert would come home from school and show his mother the red mark across his hand where the switch had snapped him back to reality. Then he would confess once again, "My head is so full of original notions that there is no vacant chamber to store away the contents of dusty books."

The teachers at Robert's school called him a day-dreamer. But if they could have looked right through his brown hair, they would have seen that inside his mind he was actually busy working on some project or other, drawing and measuring and weighing, testing this and adjusting that, until he was satisfied that everything was just right. Robert's teachers didn't even begin to guess that young Master Fulton would grow up to be a famous inventor.

But there was one person who understood Robert very well. He was a family friend named William Henry, a collector, inventor, and mechanic. Mr. Henry knew that Robert was bright and curious and liked to discover things for himself. He saw that young Fulton kept his eyes and ears open and asked questions about everything that piqued his curiosity. Mr. Henry often invited Robert home to browse among his collection of books and maps and paintings, magnets and machines, bits and pieces of clocks, and instruments that calculated the distance between stars.

Born on November 14, 1765, Robert Fulton was the next to last of five children. There were three older sisters, Betsy, Polly, and Belle, and a younger brother, Abraham. Until just a few months before Robert was born, his father had worked as a tailor in

Lancaster, Pennsylvania. But Mr. Fulton wanted to try farming instead, so he bought some land thirty miles south of town. It turned out that the soil was poor and the crops refused to grow. It wasn't long before the Fultons had to sell the land and the farmhouse with everything in it. With only the clothes they were wearing, the family moved back to Lancaster, and Robert's father took up tailoring again. Two years later, in 1774, Mr. Fulton died and Robert became the man of the house.

With the help of friends and relatives, Mrs. Fulton was able to put enough food on the table to feed her children. Her household was generally peaceful, except for an occasional outburst, like the time Robert lost his temper and threatened to beat Betsy to a pulp with the fire tongs. But warfare never lasted long before tears and hugs restored harmony. And when Robert grew tired of his brother and sisters, there were always plenty of other things to do.

Lancaster was an exciting place for a boy like Robert. It was alive with all the hustle and bustle of a growing town. It had about four thousand inhabitants, many of them Scotch-Irish Presbyterians like the Fultons. And there were always travelers passing through. Pioneers and explorers stopped in Lancaster to load up with supplies before heading west along the Conestoga Road to the territory beyond the thirteen colonies. Yet the town was only a sixty-mile wagon ride from the big city of Philadelphia.

Robert always found something interesting to occupy his time. Sometimes he joined a jeering crowd to watch the public hanging of a horse thief in the town square. On a quieter day, he might stroll down Main Street to poke his head into the library or the chemist's shop.

The chemist usually kept a supply of mercury, or quicksilver, as people sometimes called it. One of Robert's favorite pastimes was experimenting with this peculiar element. No one knows for sure exactly what Robert did with his mercury. Perhaps he poured a little into a small glass tube and watched a thin column climb upward as the day grew warmer. Or maybe he put a big drop of it on a piece of paper and shattered it into little bits with a tap of his finger. Then he might have tilted the paper this way and that and watched the tiny silver pinheads scatter every which way until, with a final shake, he brought them together again. Robert's friends called him Quicksilver Bob, because his mind moved and changed directions in a flash, just like the mercury that fascinated him so much.

One of Robert's friends, an older boy named

Christopher Hampf, used to invite him to go fishing on the Conestoga River. Although he was always happy to sink his hook into a good catch, Robert was quick to find fault with the Hampfs' boat. The poles that were used to push it forward were heavy and awkward and dripped mud all over everything. The whole arrangement was clumsy and inefficient. Robert had a better idea. He built two paddle wheels, mounted one on each side of the boat, and fitted them with hand cranks. Then as the two boys turned the cranks, the paddle wheels pushed against the water and the boat slid cleanly and quickly along. Full speed ahead, that's the way Robert liked to do things.

One of the most important events of Robert's childhood happened in 1775 when he was ten. That was the year the American Revolution began, the war that was going to bring the colonies independence from Britain and the oppressive rule of King George III. The spirit of freedom was everywhere, along with the excitement of change, the promise of self-rule, and all sorts of possibilities never before imagined. Robert's world suddenly grew from the small town where he lived into a whole new country in the making.

Lancaster became a supply center where the soldiers of America's Continental Army, under the command of General George Washington, came to stock up on guns and horses and food or to stop for a night's rest and a fresh pair of boots. Revolutionary leaders like Thomas Paine and John Hancock, Samuel and John Adams passed through on their way to meet with others in support of their cause.

Although no fighting took place in Lancaster itself, the war touched everyone. Ordinary citizens soon found that supplies were short and prices were high. The town was crowded with soldiers and prisoners and people who had fled from their homes elsewhere because of the fighting. Every day there were reports of men wounded or killed in the bloody battles of Bunker Hill and Brandywine and Freeman's Farm. The war also created new jobs for the people of Lancaster. Supporters of the Revolution published their ideas in the newspapers and shouted their beliefs from the steps of the town hall. Robert watched and listened and learned. For better or worse, these were exciting times.

②

Levers, Screws, Wedges, and Wheels

In 1781 American troops defeated the British at Yorktown in the last major battle of the war. The following year, the two sides began to work out the terms of a treaty that would turn a loosely knit cluster of thirteen colonies into a new country, the United States of America.

Robert was sixteen years old, and it was time he found work and started supporting his family. With the help of a friend, he arranged to be apprenticed to a silversmith in Philadelphia. Robert was to remain under contract for a set period of time, and in return he would learn a useful and respected trade from a master craftsman. In a few years, he would be an expert at melting and shaping silver and engraving elaborate designs on the fine serving platters and coffee urns of wealthy households.

Philadelphia was much larger than Lancaster. Robert liked the city, and his charm and dark-eyed good looks soon attracted many friends. But he didn't like working for someone else. He preferred to be master of his own thoughts and actions. More than anything else, Robert wanted success and recognition. So he soon left the silversmith and opened a shop of his own at Second and Walnut Streets, one of Philadelphia's busiest corners.

As a schoolboy back in Lancaster, Robert had liked to draw and paint with watercolors. Now, with space and time to do as he pleased, he started painting in earnest, making miniature portraits for the silver and gold lockets worn by fashionable young ladies of the day. Next he taught himself hair working, another craft that was popular at the time. With a few strands of human hair, he carefully outlined a small portrait or a spray of flowers and then framed it. Robert had the skill, the patience, and the limber fingers to excel at both hair working and miniature portrait painting.

With a little money in his pockets, he moved to an even better location, and the new shop on Front Street soon became a favorite place for Philadelphians to browse and buy.

In 1786 Robert turned twenty-one. He had finally saved enough of his earnings to make two dreams come true. First he bought a few acres of farmland in western Pennsylvania for his mother. He had wanted to do this for a long time, perhaps to make up for her disappointment when the family farm had to be sold. Then he booked passage on a transatlantic sailing ship. Robert was going to London to make a name for himself as a painter. He was hoping to study with Benjamin West, a famous American artist who lived in England.

In those days, an Atlantic crossing took weeks, often months, through rough seas, angry storms, and heavy fogs. Sails tore and food rotted. Drinking water ran low and bedbugs visited nightly. But Robert and his fellow passengers found ways to fill the time. During the days, they entertained each other with card games and storytelling. On clear nights, they stood on deck and watched the stars.

At last Robert arrived in London, a city that was more than fifteen times the size of Philadelphia. He soon discovered that decent lodging could be found in a coffeehouse for a shilling a week, and that a good set of legs and lungs could take him just about anywhere in the sprawling city. He also learned very quickly that pedestrians had better watch out for umbrellas colliding on narrow sidewalks, slops splashing from upper-story windows, and pickpockets with fingers faster than lightning. As soon as Robert had a roof over his head, he set off to find Benjamin West, a letter of introduction in his hand.

Over the next few years, Robert worked very hard at his painting and continued to seek West's advice. He moved from one lodging house to another, borrowing money when he needed it and paying it back whenever he could. He sold enough of his work to scrape by, and two of his paintings were exhibited at London's Royal Academy, which was a very great honor. But this wasn't enough for Robert. He was nearing thirty and beginning to think that perhaps painting wasn't going to bring him the success he wanted so badly.

Just about this time, an old saying proved to be true: "Necessity is the mother of invention." Many fashionable Londoners of that day hired skilled craftspeople to decorate their expensive furnishings with colorful marble inlay. Some of Robert's artist friends were very good at it. The trouble was, they complained, the tools used to cut and polish the delicate slivers of stone were clumsy at best. So Robert set to work inventing a better way to do the job. The machine he built for cutting and polishing marble became so popular that it won a silver medal from the Society for the Encouragement of Arts, Commerce, and Manufactures.

It wasn't long before Robert found other ways to use his inventive skills in the world of arts and crafts. He designed one machine that spun flax fibers into yarn, which was then woven into fabric. A variation of this idea was a device that twisted hemp into heavy rope that was far stronger than any handmade cord could ever be. Robert remembered how much he liked solving mechanical puzzles. And he never lost sight of the fact that in coming up with these tools to simplify the work of others, he was also starting to be recognized as an inventor.

Most inventors developed new machines by making models. Only after much trial and error, building and rebuilding, did they produce something that worked. But with his drawing skills, Robert could do a sketch, tear it up, and try again before making the final model, saving himself a lot of time and expense.

In his travels around England, Robert became aware of a serious problem that needed attention.

When he visited Devon and Cornwall, the rural counties southwest of London, he learned that farming conditions were very bad. The soil there was poor, but the ground was too rough to build pony trails for transporting fertilizer. The farmers worked very hard, but they lived in poverty. Without fertile soil, their crops weren't good enough to sell. Robert remembered how much his own family had suffered when their farm in Pennsylvania failed for the same reason.

Some people thought the transportation problem might be solved with a system of waterways. Horse-drawn barges could carry fertilizer and other goods from place to place with speed and efficiency. There was talk of using large-scale canals and big boats. No, said Robert. These would be too expensive to build and operate. Instead he worked out a plan for narrow canals with small boats that could be operated more economically. While others came up with bits and pieces of ideas, Robert worked out the entire design and operation of a simple and sensible canal system for all of England. He even invented a machine to dig the canals. He knew that his idea was better than any of the others and never stopped pestering people with his plans and proposals. But it wasn't until many years later, in the early 1820s, that England built its first major canal, based on a variation of Robert's design.

This was a time when Robert was thinking a lot about inventors and inventions. What did the word *invent* really mean, anyway? Some people said an invention was something completely original that no one had ever thought of before. But Robert believed that inventing meant putting old ideas together in some new combination, or taking another person's failure, finding out why it didn't work, and turning it into a success. Inventing something, he said in his own practical way, was a matter of sitting down "among levers, screws, wedges, wheels" and figuring out how to arrange them into something useful. A true inventor, said Robert, had to come up with something that worked. And that turned out to be the secret of his success.

There were plenty of skeptics who poked fun at Robert's notions and scoffed at his confidence. "They had not the sense to know the produce of genius," he complained. But that was nothing unusual. Since the beginning of time, people with new ideas had been laughed at or stoned to death or burned at the stake. Robert was fully convinced that his inventions were the best solutions to the problems he tackled. He had met a handful of others in England who thought the same way he did about progress and change, but he never managed to persuade anyone with power or money to finance his canal project. And he knew an inventor couldn't be a success unless people of influence believed in him.

And so, in June of 1797, Robert packed his belongings and set sail for France, where people were more open-minded. England had been at war with France since 1793, but a temporary lull in the fighting made travel possible. Robert planned to stay in France for about six months, but as it turned out, he was there for seven years.

3

The Boat-Fish

As Robert crossed the English Channel, he had plenty of time to think about living in France. Once again he would be in a foreign country without a single friend. Ten years before, when he had arrived in England, he'd felt the same loneliness. Now, with everyone speaking a language he didn't understand, he would be even more of a stranger.

But Robert soon forgot his worries because a new invention was taking shape in his mind. Ever since

24

his boyhood in Lancaster during the American Revolution, he had hated the idea of nations fighting each other. He felt the same way now about the war between England and France. And in addition to his personal feelings, Robert never overlooked an opportunity to promote his ideas. It was time for all war to end, he said. Robert Fulton was going to invent world peace. In doing so, of course, he planned to achieve international fame for himself.

In his head, Robert was busy working on the design of a submarine, an underwater craft that could sneak up beneath an enemy ship, plant a bomb, and then retreat to safety. The submarine was a weapon so deadly and destructive that no country would ever want to be at war again. Robert believed that when the news of his invention spread across nations and continents and oceans, people everywhere were going to see things his way. Peace would be assured, and so would his own fame and fortune.

It was important that Robert present his plan to the right people. Although France was a leading power in Europe at that time, Britain still ruled the seas. But if the French used Robert's submarine to destroy the British navy, then France would reign supreme. Robert felt no particular loyalty to the British government, which had ignored his genius, and he was sure the French would be eager to have his invention.

The idea of a submarine was not new. An American named David Bushnell had invented an underwater vessel twenty years earlier. But Bushnell couldn't get his invention to work right and eventually abandoned the project. Robert Fulton did not give up so easily.

One of Robert's most important tasks in designing a submarine was to figure out how to make it sink out of sight instead of just floating on top of the water. And it was even more important, especially if there was someone inside, to bring it back to the surface again. As usual, Robert came up with a solution. He was going to fit his submarine with storage tanks and a pump. When the tanks were filled with water, their weight would pull the sub down. When the water was pumped back out of the tanks, the submarine would return to the surface.

Then there was another important puzzle for Robert to solve. In order to approach an enemy ship, the submarine's crew had to be able to see outside. Simple, said Robert. The vessel would be fitted with small airtight windows. The crew must also monitor the ocean's surface in order to track other ships nearby. Simple again. The submarine would be equipped with a small pipe, or periscope, extending from the inside of the sub up through the hull, or body of the vessel. From their hiding place in the depths, the crew could then peer up above the surface of the water. And by turning a crank attached to the scope, they could point their viewer in any direction they wanted.

Robert was ready to start work on his new invention. But first he had to find a place to live and get to know his way around Paris. The city was a livelier place than London, and it was very much to Robert's liking.

Londoners were so serious and hardworking. They always seemed full of purpose, as if there was some place they had to be, something important they had to do. But Parisians would spend hours a day in cafés and parks, laughing and talking as if nothing else mattered. Street artists were everywhere, singing, juggling, miming. Nobody was in too much of a hurry to stop and toss a coin in a performer's hat before strolling on to watch a boat race or a costume parade. In the evenings, Parisians went to the opera or danced in brightly lit ballrooms. Back in London, upper-class gentlemen were still bowing their powdered wigs to hoopskirted ladies in a stately minuet. Here in Paris, couples were twirling around the floor, embracing each other in a daring new dance called the waltz.

Once he'd found suitable lodging, Robert was far too busy to join in all the fun. He spent the next several years improving the submarine's design and trying to interest the French government in his invention, which he called "a curious machine for mending the system of politics."

The *Nautilus,* as the submarine was named, was finally built in the early months of 1800 in a large workshop in Rouen, a town on the river Seine about eighty miles from Paris. Robert was there to oversee every step along the way as a team of blacksmiths turned the precise details of his drawings into the parts and pieces of a submarine. Each bit of metal that went into the tanks, pumps, and hull of the vessel was heated in a forge. Workers hammered the red-hot substance into rough form, then fired and hammered again until the shape and balance of each piece was exactly right.

By the summer of 1800, when Robert was thirty-four years old, he was finally ready to show his invention to the public. News of the important event spread, and crowds gathered along the banks of the river Seine near Rouen to see a demonstration of Robert Fulton's *Nautilus.* Among them was a small delegation sent by Napoleon Bonaparte, the new leader of France.

Unlike Robert, Napoleon wasn't the least bit concerned about world peace. Before taking power in 1799, he had led the French army to several victories, thus adding to France's territories. Now Napoleon wanted to extend his power even farther and was fully prepared to fight more wars if necessary.

But the spectators that day knew nothing of Napoleon's plans. Most of them were straining their eyes and ears to pick up whatever information they could about the curious gray blimp floating on the surface of the water. People in the crowd swapped ideas about how the big metal sausage was supposed to work.

The new invention was nicknamed a *bateau-poisson*, which is French for "boat-fish." According to someone in the crowd, it was going to move through the water by means of a propeller, which was operated by hand cranks inside the chamber. Once the vessel had submerged, there was supposed to be enough oxygen inside the airtight cabin for three people to breathe for up to ten hours. The bubble-shaped conning tower, fitted to the top of the hull at the front, was used for observation and entry into the main cabin.

Robert had been waiting in a rowboat beside the *Nautilus*. The crowd watched as he climbed out onto the hull, lit a candle to illuminate the dark interior of the chamber, and disappeared through the small hatch in the conning tower. His crew followed, each with a candle. The second crewman reached up to close the hatch, and within a few minutes the sub was underway, heading for a deep spot in the middle of the river.

Then without further warning, the big gray hulk sank beneath the surface and out of sight. For the first few minutes, no one spoke. Time passed and there was no sign of the sub. People watching from the shore began to whisper. It was foolish, crazy, a mad scheme, they said. Fulton and his crew would be trapped like rats.

After about twenty minutes, most of the spectators had lost hope of ever seeing the *Nautilus* again. But a few thought there was still a chance, well a small one anyway, that everything would turn out all right. After all, young Fulton was said to have a sound head on his shoulders.

Then someone shouted and a hand pointed toward the spot where the *Nautilus* had gone down. The water was bubbling. There were more shouts and more bubbles, then cheers as the slippery outline of the conning tower broke the water's surface. A few minutes later, the entire *Nautilus* was afloat and the hatch popped open. Out climbed Robert Fulton, a smile of triumph on his face.

That day, June 13, 1800, marked Robert's first big success. He was determined that many more would follow.

④

A Floating Furnace

Robert stayed in Paris and continued to fine-tune his submarine, still hoping that the French government would take an interest in it. In December of 1801, he met a wealthy and important man named Robert Livingston. About twenty years older than Fulton, Livingston was already a well-known figure in American politics. He had helped to write the Declaration of Independence and later served as President Washington's secretary of foreign affairs.

He was now the American ambassador to France, newly appointed by President Thomas Jefferson. Like Robert, Livingston had a very lively imagination and thought of himself as an inventor. Unlike Robert, however, he didn't know how to put his ideas down on paper, nor did he have the mechanical skills to produce anything.

When Robert Livingston met Robert Fulton soon after Livingston's arrival in Paris, he suspected that the young man's talents might prove useful to him. As the two men talked together, Fulton boasted about the new submarine that was going to bring world peace. That was all very fine, the older man agreed, but he himself was more interested in a project closer to home, a steamboat that would carry passengers and freight on the Hudson River between New York City and Albany.

At that time, many riverboats were powered by sails or drawn by horses along tow paths. A few people were experimenting with steam engines, but so far the results were clumsy and slow. Livingston knew that the inventor of a steamboat that was fast and efficient would become rich and famous. When he asked Robert to work with him on the Hudson River project, the young inventor accepted the challenge without hesitation. Robert also believed in the future of the steam-powered boat, and he was sure he could build a good one.

In a frenzy of excitement, Robert began drawing plans. He was so sure of his eventual success that he didn't even worry about keeping his new invention a secret. He talked endlessly about his project and savored the attention it brought him.

Considering and rejecting various ideas, Robert soon decided that the best possible device for propelling the boat was a paddle wheel. In developing his plans further, he knew that he must keep in mind two important properties of water. One property was that water offers resistance and tends to slow down an object moving through it. So the shape of the hull had to be streamlined to allow the boat to glide easily. The other important point was that water will eventually give way to a moving object. Therefore, as Robert explained to anyone willing to listen, the paddles must have enough push, or thrust, to move the boat forward and not simply spin in place.

Robert worked on the design of the steamboat until the end of 1802, sketching, modifying, improving, and experimenting with small-scale models. The final version, he reported to Livingston, was going to be 6 feet wide and 90 feet long. It would travel at eight miles per hour upstream, covering the 140 miles from New York City to Albany in only eighteen hours. Calculations spilled from Robert's head onto scraps of paper. The boat would take about 50 passengers, he figured, and each trip would clear nearly two hundred dollars. Yes, indeed, a good profit. "Without vanity," he told Livingston, "I think I am perfect master of the details."

It wasn't long before Robert's original plan began to grow. If he built a longer boat and made a few improvements in the design, he could move it upstream at twelve miles an hour and carry 120 passengers. He could charge a lower fare and still make a good profit. A few days later, Robert came up with a way to increase the speed to sixteen miles per hour. Some of his friends thought that Fulton, poor fellow, had lost his mind.

With the help of a shipbuilder named Mr. Périer, who had helped Robert to construct the *Nautilus,* and a mechanical engineer named Etienne Calla, Robert began construction of his new steamboat. Périer and Calla were to work on the engine. Robert himself would build the two paddle wheels and the hull. The hull had to be strong enough to hold its own against the pounding of the steam-driven engine, a force greater than the hammering of a storm on the high seas.

In May of 1803, the project was completed. The boat measured 56½ feet long and 10½ feet wide, somewhat smaller than the original plan. It was flat bottomed and sharply pointed at the bow and stern, or front and back, for low resistance and high speed. The boiler, which produced the steam, sat beside the engine just about midship, on top of the heavy wooden planks that formed the deck. The two paddle wheels, each with ten blades, were attached on either side of the hull. The whole thing was steered by a rudder, a large piece of wood shaped like a fish tail and attached to the stern. To control the rudder, a small wooden handle called a tiller was positioned on the inside of the boat.

People stared and pointed at the funny looking structure tied up along the banks of the Seine. Some of them laughed and said it looked like a floating furnace. But others thought that this amazing new invention might turn out to be a success. Among them were a few of the barge captains who made their living carrying cargo on the river. These men saw the boat as a threat, a dangerous competitor that might even put them out of business some day.

One night not long before the big demonstration was to take place, a messenger wakened Robert from a sound sleep to report that his steamboat had sunk.

Newspapers said that vandals had slashed the hull, but no one was sure what really happened. Robert worked the rest of that night, all the next day, and into the following night, tugging and pulling with ropes and weights and muscles to rescue the boiler and engine. He managed to save the boat's machinery. But the hull was damaged beyond repair.

For the next two months, Robert spent all his waking hours building a new hull. He modified the design again to make a more streamlined boat measuring 74½ feet long and 8 feet wide. By the time the new hull was ready, the boiler and engine had been restored to perfect working order. Robert had put so much of his energy and worry into the new boat that he thought of it as his own child. "My boy, who is all bones and corners just like his daddy," he told a friend, "and whose birth has given me much uneasiness, or rather anxiety, is just learning to walk and I hope in time he will be an active runner."

The trial run of the steamboat was scheduled for late in the day on August 9. The summer sun lingered well into the evening and provided plenty of light for the show. Earlier in the day, Robert began tossing logs into the boiler. The fire had to be good and hot in order to produce enough steam to operate the giant paddle wheels.

A newspaper reporter arrived on the scene early and scribbled notes on his pad, searching for words to describe the sight before him, a cross between a boat and a chariot and a fire engine. By six o'clock, a crowd of Parisians had turned out for the first performance of Mr. Fulton's steamboat.

Many of the city's socialites were there, dressed to the nines for the occasion. Among them stood dock workers in dirty overalls and beggars in rags. Some had seen the *Nautilus*. Others had only heard about Robert Fulton's inventions. Some were believers, others scoffed. Some shouted and cheered as they heard the first hiss of steam in the cylinder. Others secretly hoped for something more exciting. Perhaps the boiler would burst into flames. Or better yet, maybe the whole cockeyed contraption would blow up before their very eyes. Now that would be worth watching!

The sounds and smells from the engine were familiar to everyone who knew about the steam-operated factory on the other side of town. But when the two paddle wheels began to turn, slowly pushing the boat forward through the water, the crowd stared in disbelief. They had all seen barges towed upriver by horses and mules. But a boat that moved by itself was quite another matter.

With his crew of three and a handful of invited guests on board, Robert steered the steamboat upstream. It started at a cautious speed of three miles per hour, then puffed and splashed its way as high as four and a half. From their straight course up the middle of the river, the paddle wheels churned up waves big enough to roll all the way to shore.

The demonstration lasted an hour and a half. The following day, a Paris newspaper proclaimed the new invention a complete and brilliant success. Fulton's steamboat, the article said, would be able to carry cargo to and from the commercial wharves of the big city in one-tenth the time that it took a horse-drawn barge.

But even as the good news began to spread, Robert was already planning improvements in the hull and the machinery. His boat would have to steam along much faster before he himself would be satisfied with it.

⑤

The Devil in a Sawmill

Following the trial of his new steamboat in Paris, Robert returned to England to finish up some business. It had finally become obvious that no one in the French government wanted his submarine. Frustrated, Robert turned right around and offered his deadly weapon to Britain, which was still competing with France for control of the seas. But in 1805, the British navy defeated the French fleet once and for all at the Battle of Trafalgar. After that, no government had any further interest in a submarine. Robert was very annoyed that all his hard work had been for nothing. His invention hadn't made any contribution to world peace. Nor had it brought him the recognition he wanted.

In December of 1806, Robert returned to America, twenty years after he had left home to become a famous painter. He was now in his early forties. Robert Livingston had also come home, to Clermont, his country estate on the Hudson, and the two men decided to go ahead with the Hudson River project. The partnership, however, was to be a stormy one. Both men looked forward to the success of their company, but they disagreed on such things as who was to pay the start-up costs, who was to take what percentage of the profits, and what changes should be made in the design of the steamboats. Written contracts between them were lost and oral agreements misunderstood. Never mind. The important thing was that the project was underway.

Even though the Paris steamboat had gotten a lot of attention a few years earlier, no one ever thought much more about it. It was a curiosity, everyone said, a crazy experiment that just happened to work for an hour or two. Well, Robert Fulton would show them. Once again he was setting out to impress the world with a new invention, and this time people were going to take it seriously.

New York City was a promising place for an inventor like Robert to peddle his wares. It was a major port, its harbor held as many as five hundred boats, and its two rivers, the Hudson and the East, bustled with the business of international trade. Robert found comfortable lodging in a boardinghouse on Broadway. Then, in a busy neighborhood of shipyards and docks along the East River, he met a builder named Charles Browne who agreed to make the boat's hull.

The new steamboat began to take shape in the spring of 1807. It was warm enough to do most of the sawing and assembling outdoors. Robert worked right alongside Mr. Browne's carpenters. Every detail had to be just so, every joint and pinning and shaping finely tuned. Although Robert was a stern master, his men never complained. He encouraged them and praised their work. They were as eager as he was to build the first boat to steam up the Hudson. In fact Robert was far more gentlemanly toward his workers than he was toward his partner, whose suggestions he often dismissed with his usual arrogance.

Sometimes at the end of a long day, Robert scribbled a quick note to Livingston, who was relaxing upriver at Clermont. He had decided to modify the design of the hull, he reported, keeping a narrow width of 13 feet and extending the length to 150 feet.

The sides of the hull were to be 5 feet high at the deck, rising straight up from a flat bottom. A small cabin with 2 added feet of height would be roomy enough for a 6-footer like Robert to stand comfortably with his hat on. The design of the boat, he assured Livingston, allowed for the movement of the tides and the usual dangers of river navigation.

As for profits, a matter that was always on both men's minds, Robert figured the boat was big enough to take fifty paying passengers. They could probably make four trips between New York City and Albany each week, forty weeks a year, allowing for the three winter months when the river froze over. Figuring in the cost of coal to fuel the engine, plus food and bedding for the passengers, they could expect a handsome profit of $32,000 a year.

By the end of May, the steamboat's hull had its first coat of paint. It was then moved to another shipyard along the East River, where the boat's machinery was to be added. By the second week in July, the engine, designed by Englishmen Matthew Boulton and James Watt, was retrieved from the customs warehouse, uncrated, assembled, and installed. A huge crosswise axle connected and secured the two paddle wheels.

The day of departure came on August 17, when the *Steamboat,* as Fulton and Livingston called it, was to begin its journey up the Hudson. The boat was docked only a few miles from New York's city hall. A crowd watched from the wharf, laughing and buzzing about the silly contrivance that was preparing to plow through the water with its giant arms. They called it "Fulton's Folly."

Livingston had invited, or rather ordered, a handful of friends and family to ride on the maiden voyage. Most of them were afraid for their lives. And even if by some miracle they survived the trip, they would be laughed at for taking part in such a reckless adventure. But Livingston was a persuasive and powerful man, and no one dared refuse him. Even Robert, who didn't like the idea of turning the trial run of the steamboat into a big party, let Livingston have his way.

The guests, dressed in their best ruffles and bonnets, were wined and dined in high style. Just before the mooring lines were cast off from the pier, Robert stood to greet the passengers. "My friends were in groups on the deck," he remembered later. "There was anxiety mixed with fear among them. They were silent, sad, and weary. I read in their looks nothing but disaster."

A handful of the passengers cheered as the boat pulled away from the dock and pointed upstream.

Robert watched as faces began to relax. A few of the guests chattered to each other in amazement. Some sat staring down into the water, hypnotized by the rhythmic slapping of the paddles. Others held on to the railing and gazed across at the high cliffs that commanded the Hudson.

While the steamboat chugged upriver at a speed of about five miles per hour, Robert was occupied with the rumblings of the engine and the hissings of the boiler, alert to any sound that might mean trouble. Along the shore, farmers and villagers scattered in panic at the sight of the fire-puffing monster that appeared out of the mist. They thought it was the devil making his way up the river in a sawmill.

The next day the steamboat docked at Clermont, 110 miles upriver, for lunch. Even though his relationship with Robert Fulton had been difficult, Livingston was obviously enjoying the importance of the occasion when he stood to address his guests. This was a day of triumph, he said, marking one of the great events of history.

Word spread fast. The maiden voyage of Fulton's steamboat, which came to be called the *North River Steamboat of Clermont*—or simply the *Clermont*—was a success. It still didn't go as fast as Robert might have liked, but no one else seemed to mind.

A few passengers, then handfuls, then dozens bought tickets for the next run from New York City to Albany, even though many people believed that the first trip was just a lucky accident. As one adventurous young gentleman, a Quaker named John Wilson, stepped on board, a friend called after him, "John, will thee risk thy life in such a concern? I tell thee she is the most fearful wild fowl living, and thy father ought to restrain thee!" But the second journey upriver and the many that followed finally convinced the American public that the age of the steamboat had arrived.

6

The Fire Canoe

Robert, still a bachelor, was now in his forties and considered a very good catch. He was tall and handsome. A hint of an English accent heightened his already charming manner. He had the pride of a self-made man and the polish of a man of the world. He dressed tastefully in fine shirts, fashionable waistcoats, cashmere breeches, and silk stockings. Now that fame and fortune were at last within his reach, it was time for him to think about starting a family. Robert had fallen in love with Livingston's young cousin Harriet, and they were married on January 7, 1808.

Changes all around the country were keeping pace with the new events in Robert's life. Thomas Jefferson, now in his second term as president, was a man who looked to the future and encouraged new ideas. During Jefferson's first term, with the Louisiana Purchase of 1803, the United States had acquired from France a huge tract of land between the Mississippi River and the Rocky Mountains. The next year, Jefferson had sent Meriwether Lewis and William Clark on an expedition to explore the western lands and rivers and to look for possible trade routes to the Pacific Ocean.

The Mississippi River was the gateway to the western territories and the key to westward expansion. Jefferson wasn't the only one interested in the river's great potential. Even before Robert returned to America, he had thought about the possibility of steamboat navigation on the Mississippi. The Hudson was a challenge, of course, but a small one compared to the great Father of Waters, a much larger river in every way—wider, longer, more powerful, more treacherous.

Robert paid close attention to the information that Lewis and Clark had gathered, especially what they said about the force of the Mississippi currents, the hazards of snags and sandbars, and the quantities and kinds of goods being traded. Their reports helped him to predict the possible risks and rewards of developing steamboat traffic on the river. Never satisfied, Robert still dreamed of a venture that would impress the world, and it seemed to him that this one was made to order.

Robert designed a Mississippi steamboat but soon realized he would not have time to oversee its construction. The Hudson River fleet was growing so fast that he was now a businessman as well as an inventor and builder. He would have to entrust the Mississippi project to someone else. Robert hired a young boatbuilder named Nicholas Roosevelt and found a suitable shipyard in Pittsburgh along the banks of the Monongahela River. Timbers for the hull were sawed by hand, hauled through the woods, and rafted down the Monongahela to the shipyard. The engine was ordered from Boulton and Watt in England.

By the fall of 1811, the new steamboat was ready. It was named the *New Orleans* after the city that was to be its home port. There were fifteen on board for the maiden voyage, among them Nicholas and his pregnant wife, Lydia. Lydia's friends were shocked that she was going along. Steamboat travel was still very risky, after all, especially for a woman in her condition. Her father thought the Mississippi River was the end of the earth, the point beyond which a person fell off the civilized world. But Lydia wasn't about to miss the adventure of a lifetime.

The September sun warmed friends and family as they waved the *New Orleans* out of sight. Robert stood on the riverbank with them, proud and confident. Although the others didn't say anything, the same fear was in everyone's mind. They might never see the boat or its passengers again. As the *New Orleans* steamed along past the wooded banks of the Monongahela and into the larger Ohio River, Indians peered from behind the trees at the smoke-spewing fire canoe, the dragon boat bearing down on them.

Soon the day came for the *New Orleans* to flex her muscles as she neared the big rapids just below Louisville. The pilot, Mr. Andrew Jack, stood in the bow barking orders at the helmsman. His eyes were trained on the gray foaming water, alert for any clues to the all-important difference between a mere swirl of the current and a jagged rock waiting just beneath the murky surface to slash the hull to bits. The *New Orleans* came through the rapids without so much as a scratch, and Mr. Fulton's boat steamed on into the Mississippi. Everyone on board knew they were heading into an unpredictable giant of a river, whose moods could be quiet or stormy, gentle or savage.

Sound asleep in their cabin one night, the Roosevelts awoke with a start to the jangle of the ship's bell. Within just seconds steam hissed, valves clanked, and paddle blades splashed. The *New Orleans* was underway.

Far louder than the familiar noises of the boat coming to life was a terrifying, sinister sound, a sound beyond imagination. It was the grinding and tearing of the earth as huge chunks of riverbank ripped away and twisting trees crashed into the swirling river. Mr. Jack said it was an earthquake. No one spoke. Tiger, the Roosevelt's big Newfoundland dog, paced the deck and growled.

The tremors continued for three days. In the calm that followed the quake, the crew saw an entire island swept away by the current and a whole town swallowed up by gaping holes in the earth. But Robert's boat had proved a match for the pounding, churning wreckage that slashed at her hull, and shortly after noon on January 10, 1812, the *New Orleans* prepared to dock at its home port. "Round her to," shouted Nicholas from the helm. "Lower the fires." Standing at the rail next to him was Lydia, holding their newborn daughter.

The pier was jammed with people waving flags and handkerchiefs to cheer the arrival of the first Mississippi steamboat, survivor of the worst earthquake ever known in that part of the world. Everyone in the crowd knew that they would see more of Mr. Fulton's steamboats on the Mississippi in the years to come.

Robert kept busy with new ideas and inventions. Within two years of the maiden voyage of the *New Orleans,* he had fourteen paddle wheelers steaming along on North American rivers and lakes all the way from Canada to the Gulf of Mexico. The War of 1812 between Britain and the United States rekindled Robert's earlier interest in building a steam-powered battleship, and this too kept him well occupied. A new age of industry and technology was just around the corner, and Americans saw Robert Fulton as the man who could make their country a leader in the coming revolution.

The Fultons had settled comfortably into a small house on Harriet's family estate. There, overlooking the Hudson, just a few miles from Clermont, they raised their family, three daughters and a son.

One winter day in 1815, Robert and his lawyer Mr. Emmet were returning from a business trip to Jersey City. They had to cross the frozen Hudson to get back to New York. Although the ferries weren't running, they managed to hire a small boat to take them back. As the two men were walking on a patch of frozen river to get to the boat, the ice broke and Emmet fell into the water. Robert splashed into the dark slush and pulled him out. Emmet survived the dunking, but Robert suffered severe exposure. He died soon afterward, on the morning of Thursday, February 23.

Representatives of the state and national governments joined a crowd of thousands on the banks of the Hudson to pay their last respects to a man of genius, and to watch a procession of steamboats and battleships honoring the great American inventor. In the lead was an exact reproduction of the *North River Steamboat of Clermont.*

Robert was only forty-nine years old when he died, but he had achieved the fame he had always wanted. And with his characteristic lack of modesty, he attributed his success as an inventor entirely to himself. There's no telling what other crazy notions might have come into Robert Fulton's head if he had lived out his full life.

Bibliography

Botkin, B. A., ed. *A Treasury of Mississippi River Folklore.* New York: Crown Publishers, 1978.

Dickinson, Henry W. *Robert Fulton, Engineer and Artist, His Life and Works.* Freeport, N.Y.: Books for Libraries Press, 1971.

Firestone, Clark B. *Flowing South.* New York: Robert M. McBride and Company, 1941.

Foster, Genevieve. *The Year of the Horseless Carriage, 1801.* New York: Scribner, 1975.

Morgan, John S. *Robert Fulton.* New York: Mason/Charter, 1977.

Morrison, John Harrison. *History of American Steam Navigation.* New York: Stephen Daye Press, 1958.

Philip, Cynthia Owen. *Robert Fulton, a Biography.* New York: Franklin Watts, 1985.

Virginskii, V. S. *Robert Fulton, 1765–1815.* New Delhi: Amerind Publishing Co. for the Smithsonian Institution and the National Science Foundation, 1976.

Index